TRENT DIMAS

A Real-Life Reader Biography

Valerie Menard
Sue Boulais

Mitchell Lane Publishers, Inc.
P.O. Box 200 • Childs, Maryland 21916

Second Printing

Real-Life Reader Biographies

Selena	Robert Rodriguez	Mariah Carey	Rafael Palmeiro
Tommy Nuñez	**Trent Dimas**	Cristina Saralegui	Andres Galarraga
Oscar De La Hoya	Gloria Estefan	Jimmy Smits	Mary Joe Fernandez
Cesar Chavez	Sinbad	Vanessa Williams	Paula Abdul
Celine Dion	Chuck Norris	Sammy Sosa	Brandy
Shania Twain	Mia Hamm	Garth Brooks	Jeff Gordon

Library of Congress Cataloging-in-Publication Data
Menard, Valerie.
    Trent Dimas / Valerie Menard, Sue Boulais.
        p. cm. — (A real-life reader biography)
    Includes index.
    Summary: Presents a biography of the first American gymnast of Latino heritage to win an Olympic gold medal.
    ISBN 1-883845-50-5 (lib. bdg.)
    1. Dimas, Trent, 1970– —Juvenile literature. 2. Gymnasts—United States—Biography—Juvenile literature. 3. Hispanic Americans—Biography—Juvenile literature. [1. Dimas, Trent, 1970– 2. Gymnasts. 3. Hispanic Americans--Biography.] I. Boulais, Sue. II. Title. III. Series.
GV460.2.D56M46   1997
796.44'092--dc21
[B]
                                      97-21984
                                         CIP
                                         AC

ABOUT THE AUTHORS: Valerie Menard has been an editor for *Hispanic* magazine since the magazine moved to Austin, Texas, from Washington, D.C. in July 1994. She was previously a managing editor of a bilingual weekly, *La Prensa*. As a journalist, Valerie writes from a Latino perspective and as an advocate for Latino causes. She is the author of several stories for children. **Sue Boulais** is a freelance writer and editor based in Orlando, Florida. She has published numerous books, including **Famous Astronauts** (Media Materials) and **Hispanic American Achievers** (Frog Publications). Previously, she served as an editor for *Weekly Reader* and Harcourt Brace.

PHOTO CREDITS: cover, courtesy Trent Dimas; p. 4 sketch by Barbara Tidman; pp. 6, 8, 9, 11, 15, 19 courtesy Trent Dimas; p. 20 Reuters/Michael Probst/Archive Photos; p. 22 Reuters/Wolfgang Rattay/Archive Photos; pp. 23, 25, 26, 28, 29 courtesy Trent Dimas

ACKNOWLEDGMENTS: The following story is an authorized biography. It is based on author Valerie Menard's personal interviews with Trent Dimas. It has been approved for publication by Trent Dimas. Our sincerest appreciation goes to Trent and his wife, Lisa for the time they spent with Valerie and for supplying personal photographs.

Table of Contents

Chapter 1
Getting Started

Trent Dimas was born in Albuquerque, New Mexico, on November 10, 1970. His father, Ted Sr., a former amateur boxing champion, worked as a masonry contractor. His mother, Bonnie Rivera Dimas, stayed at home during his early years, but later she worked as a hotel manager. Trent has a brother, Ted Jr., who is two years older.

Trent and his family are very close.

Trent and his family are very close. He remembers: "My parents have always looked after us very well; they never let us out of their

Trent at 5 months old

sight. They spent a lot of time with us daily, not just on the weekends."

Bonnie and Ted decided to educate Ted Jr. and Trent at home. Trent's father taught them math and science, while his mother taught them English and social studies; they continued to do so until Ted was ready for high school and Trent entered seventh grade.

Bonnie and Ted Sr. saw to it, however, that the boys participated in community sports programs so that they could meet and learn to get along with other children of the same age. Trent says, "Our parents wanted to make sure we were having fun and staying out of trouble while we made friends."

He began his gymnastics career at the age of five, along with Ted Jr., who was seven. Coached by their parents, the boys also began playing soccer together. For several years, Trent and Ted competed in both sports. Then, one year, the state soccer championships and the state gymnastics meet were on the same weekend. To compete in both events was impossible. "Our parents let us make the decision," Trent remembers. "We picked gymnastics."

Trent feels he liked gymnastics more because it's considered an individual sport. The athlete is more responsible for his own success. He says, "Gymnastics encourages discipline. It encourages

He began his gym-nastics career at the age of five.

you to set goals and to learn to overcome adversity [something that works against you], whether it's physical pain or mental weakness."

To make sure the boys could compete in gymnastics, their parents made many sacrifices. They also constantly supported and encouraged both boys. Says Trent in admiration and appreciation, "My parents were

Ted (left), age 8, and Trent (right) age 6, taken at Easter time, 1977

always with us, at competitions, at school, everywhere. They also made it clear that they would support whatever we wanted to do, but that we couldn't quit once we started. We had to finish."

His parents' support became especially important when Trent began high school. By then, Trent knew what his goal was: to be a member of the U.S. men's gymnastics team.

The Dimas family in 1981. Ted Sr., Bonnie, Ted Jr. (front) and Trent.

Chapter 2
Practice Makes Perfect

Trent's school years were filled with gymnastics practice.

Trent's high school years were filled with gymnastics practice, practice, practice. A male gymnast must be able to perform perfectly on five different pieces of gymnastic equipment (pommel horse, still rings, vault, parallel bars, and horizontal or high bar). He also has to complete a perfect series of floor exercises.

On the floor exercise, a gymnast's positions and movements come

from acrobatics, ballet, and
tumbling: short runs, soaring leaps,
full-body and leg swings, twists,
flips, handstands, handsprings,
somersaults. Most movements can
be performed forward or backward,
in double or triple combinations,
with or without hand support.

*Trent could
perform for the
camera, too.*

For his performance on each
piece of equipment, a gymnast
must create a routine lasting from

30 to 70 seconds—except for the vault, which lasts only a few seconds. In each routine, the gymnast must include several acrobatic moves, and he must perform them quickly and smoothly. On some pieces of equipment, the gymnast must perform hold positions for two to three seconds. On other pieces of equipment, he must perform releases—taking both hands off the bars, then regrasping the bars without stopping. In some routines, he may be required to reverse his swing. And a good gymnast must "stick" his final landing—come off the equipment and hit the mat solidly on both feet with no steps or hops forward or backward.

Trent trained hard to perfect the physical skills he needed. The muscles in his back, shoulders, and

Trent trained hard to perfect the physical skills he needed.

arms became very strong and flexible. He perfected his balance and the coordination of his arm and leg movements so that he could perform routines gracefully and effortlessly. He built up his strength and endurance.

Trent trained his mind, too. At times, he didn't think that he could win. But he worked hard to control his doubts so that they wouldn't hurt his confidence. He concentrated on seeing himself as a winning Olympic gymnast, going over every movement and routine in his mind.

Trent's practice paid off. He won many medals in national and international competitions. He won recognition in men's gymnastics. In fact, by the time Trent was ready for college, he was America's top male gymnast recruit!

Trent trained his mind, too. Sometimes he didn't think he could win.

Trent enrolled at the University of Nebraska.

"I was the number one recruit [in gymnastics] and had my choice of any college in the United States that had a gymnastics program," Trent explains. He chose to go to the University of Nebraska, where his brother, Ted, was already attending on a full athletic scholarship.

Trent enrolled at the university, planning to earn a marketing degree. He also joined Ted on the university's gymnastics team. In 1990, he led the team to the NCAA championships. At the end of that year, however, Trent faced another decision, one that he had to think hard about.

"I remember watching [another gymnast] . . . and I thought, 'Wow, this is the guy who I trained with for so many years, and he's really surpassing [going ahead of] me in skill. What am I going to have to do

Ted and Trent were together on the gymnastics team at the University of Nebraska.

in the next two years to make that Olympic team?"

Trent decided to leave the University of Nebraska. "I thought that the best way to make the Olympic team would be to have a couple of good athletes in the gym and more one-on-one coaching." So Trent returned to Albuquerque and started two years of intense, full-time training at his hometown gymnasium, the Gold Cup Gymnastics School. He really wanted to make the U.S. Olympic Gymnastics Team.

He really wanted to make the U.S. Olympic Gymnastics Team.

Chapter 4
Gold Medal Gymnast

Two years later, Trent achieved his goal when he qualified for the U.S. Men's Gymnastic Team during tryouts. However, his achievement wasn't as perfect as he had dreamed it would be.

When Trent left the University of Nebraska in 1990, he was a leading U.S. male gymnast. In 1992, when he arrived in Barcelona, Spain, for the Olympics, his reputation had slipped to that of a "dark horse." A

Two years later, Trent qualified for the team.

"dark horse" is a contestant whose ability or skill isn't well known.

Trent hadn't trained with a U.S. gymnastics team or coach. Just before the Olympic tryouts, he had injured himself, and nobody had expected him to qualify. Although he had qualified, he was placed fairly low on the team: fifth place out of a seven-man team.

His order of performance in the Olympic competitions worked against him, too. He was the first to compete in almost every event. That meant that usually he was sent out to provide the base score for everyone else to top.

However, Trent refused to let any of this get him down. He was very happy about competing in Barcelona. He had accomplished his goal: he had made the Olympic team. He, Trent Dimas, was an

Just before the tryouts, Trent was hurt. No one expected him to qualify.

Olympic gymnast! A medal would just be icing on the cake.

When Trent stepped up to perform on the horizontal bar, he wasn't sure what kind of performance he could deliver. Nervousness had kept him awake

Trent performs a vault for the U.S. Olympic team.

for the two nights before the event. He had never won a major international competition. At least he was competing on his favorite piece of equipment.

However, he knew what kind of performance he wanted to turn in. So, for a heartbeat, he closed his eyes and pictured in his mind a perfect routine—exactly. Then he leaped up, grasped the horizontal bar—and *did it*: a spectacular 30-second flight of back flips, swings, heart-stopping releases and unbelievable catches, a final triple backward somersault into a fabulous landing—which he stuck.

He knew it was the best routine he'd ever performed.

"My body was doing the work," Trent remembers, "and my mind was off in another world, saying, 'I can't believe this is happening.'"

As he raised his hand to signal the end of his routine, his face broke into a huge smile. He knew it was the best routine he'd ever performed. "After I stuck the dismount, I didn't want to move," he said. "I wanted to make sure the judges saw that I had stuck my routine." They certainly had—and rewarded him with a score of 9.875 (a score of 10 is perfect) and an Olympic gold medal.

Trent, with coach Ed Burch, stares in disbelief as his scores indicate he's won a gold medal.

Trent celebrates his victory in the individual high bar competition on August 2 at the XXV Summer Olympics.

With that performance, Trent became the first U.S. gymnast to win a gold medal in a nonboycotted Olympics in 60 years. He is the first, and is still the only, American

gymnast, male or female, to win a gold medal in an Olympic Games that was not held in the United States. He also became a hero to his teammates, giving the team its only Olympic medal. Ed Burch, Trent's coach, said about the men's gymnastics program, "We've been put down a lot. We needed a hero like Trent."

Trent closes his eyes and smiles as The Star Spangled Banner *is sung.*

Chapter 5
Working with Others

After the 1992 Olympics, Trent retired from gymnastics. For several years, he made endorsements, promotions, and personal appearances, and he headed gymnastics clinics for many large corporations such as Kodak, McDonald's, IBM, Xerox, AT&T, and Visa.

Painful, serious injuries kept Trent from qualifying for the 1996 Olympic Games in Atlanta,

"LAUGH AT GRAVITY. REMEMBER YOUR TRAINING. MAKE ADJUSTMENTS. TAKE A CHANCE. USE GREAT FILM. EMBRACE DESTINY."

WHAT FILM IS IN YOUR CAMERA?

CHRIS COLE ON PHOTOGRAPHING TRENT DIMAS, '92 OLYMPICS

Georgia. Fortunately, though, his injuries didn't stop his wedding. On December 29, 1996, he married Lisa Harris, his girlfriend of many years.

Trent and Lisa, with Lisa's father, at their wedding reception

Much of Trent's work now is with young people. Youth groups, corporations, and charities often invite Trent to speak. He truly enjoys being a role model because he feels that there's a lack of them.

Trent devotes a great deal of time to Children's Hospice International, an organization that works with terminally ill children. "Working with these kids and seeing how their lives are—it can really bring you back to Earth," he explains. ". . . These kids are just looking forward to that one day that's not perfect, but just completely normal."

Trent participates in programs sponsored by the U.S. Olympic Committee. In one such program, he discusses violence and suicide among young people. In another, he tours schools nationwide and encourages students to work toward participation in the Olympics.

Trent was the first American gymnast of Latino descent to win an Olympic medal.

As the first American gymnast of Latino descent to win an Olympic medal, Trent is also involved in activities that help other young Latinos. He's a spokesman for the National Hispanic Scholarship Fund (NHSF). "The NHSF gives ninety-five percent of the funds that they raise to the students who need it most," he states. Trent himself sponsors five college scholarships for deserving Latino students through the NHSF.

After his Olympic victory, Trent visited with President George Bush and the first lady.

He worries that few young Latinos compete in junior gymnastics programs. "Gymnastics is a progressive sport, and to be an elite gymnast, one has to begin training early in life. . . . In order for more Hispanics to be in the Games, more must train hard, with the

TRENT DIMAS

Trent continues as a host, fund-raiser, and speaker for many events.

focus of being in an Olympic Games as a primary goal."

Trent intends to work in television, perhaps producing Olympic sporting events. However, he also wants to continue his work with young people. At times he carries his gold medal with him to inspire the children he meets to believe in their dreams. He wants to help them understand that if they work hard and are dedicated and have goals, what happened for him can happen for them. He tells them, "There's going to be a lot of things in your way along the road. My mom used to always tell me that for every no there's a yes, and you have to keep knocking on doors until you find where that yes is."

If the past is any indication, Trent Dimas will keep knocking on doors—and finding the yes.

Trent carries his gold medal with him to inspire the children he meets to believe in their dreams.

Chronology

- Born November 10, 1970, in Albuquerque, New Mexico; mother: Bonnie Rivera; father: Ted Dimas Sr.
- Educated at home until seventh grade
- 1975, took first gymnastics class
- 1989, graduated from El Dorado High School in Albuquerque
- 1989–1990, attended University of Nebraska
- 1990, member of NCAA National Championship gymnastics team
- 1992, qualified for the U.S. gymnastics team; won gold medal in individual high bar event, August 2
- 1992, retired from gymnastics
- 1996, married Lisa Harris
- Continues today as speaker and host for many events

Index